A Snack for GRACK

by Kristi Holl

Chapter One

"My back hurts," Willox Wuzford groaned, shifting the large bag of fur caps strapped to his shoulders.

"Stop grumbling," said his mom, smiling. "You know everyone on Planet Globius has to pick fur caps, or those weeds would destroy our crops."

Suddenly, a silver spaceship flashed across the sky and landed directly in front of them! A door slid open, something tumbled out, and Will gasped. Smiling up at him was the oddest creature he had ever seen.

Will found a note tied to its neck. "Enjoy this flizzard, a gift from the planet Vandor. Flizzards eat—"

Just then, the creature grabbed the note and gobbled it down.

Chapter Two

Will and his mom took the flizzard home, bringing the spaceship for it to live in.

"Grack!" the creature squawked happily, naming itself.

"Now let's find out what it eats," said Willox's dad. He tried healthy foods like fuzz fruit, nubnuts, and bling cheese, but Grack spit them all out.

"What about Globby-Goo?" Will asked, holding out one of the sweet, sticky bars.

"Those are nothing but sugar," Mom said, horrified.

But Grack snapped it up, and from then on, he would eat nothing else.

Chapter Three

Grack grew bigger and rounder on his Globby-Goo diet. Soon it was impossible for him to fly.

One day, Will was picking fur caps when a screech ripped through the air.

"GRA-A-A-A-CK!!"

"Grack's in trouble!" cried Will. He raced home to find Grack stuck in his doorway. Will dropped to his knees and began tugging.

Chapter Four

Suddenly, Grack jammed his face into Will's fur cap bag and started munching.

"You like these awful-tasting fur caps?" Will asked. Backing up, he held out one of the plants.

Grack groaned, puffed, and wiggled, until he popped out of the doorway. Immediately, he gulped down the fur cap.

After that, Grack practically lived in the fields, feasting on fur caps. His healthy diet soon had him back in shape and flying high, and no one ever had to pick fur caps again!